Anger Management

A Step By Step Guide That Teaches You How To Take Charge Of Your Emotions, Simplify Your Thought Process, Put An End To Excessive Overthinking, And Become More Skilled In Relationships And Social

Renato Bautista

TABLE OF CONTENT

Be Dedicated To Finding A Solution To The Issue 1

You Should Not Underestimate The Risk That Comes With Being Angry. 8

The Experience Of Victimization Leads To A Loss Of Agency 16

Learn How To Settle Your Nerves. 30

Alterations To One's Way Of Life May Help In Anger Management. 34

Figure Out How To Keep Yourself In Check 49

A Calm State Can Easily Be Maintained If You Follow These Easy Steps 53

Meditation: Don't Take It Personally 61

The Effects That Feeling Angry Has On Our Children 69

Why Some People Become More Angry Than Others And What Causes It. 86

Defining The Different Stages Of Development 98

Revealing Your Own Personal Manner Of Anger 102

Anger That Is Both Loud And Noisy 110

Why Is This Person So Angry?............................ 117

Anger That Is Channeled In A Positive Way . 151

You Can Help Your Children Better Manage Their Anger By Teaching Them Self-Control.
.... 157

Advancing One Step Further: The Effects And Cautionary Notes.. 168

Be Dedicated To Finding A Solution To The Issue

If you find that expressing your anger, particularly against those you care about, causes you excruciating pain and leaves you feeling alone and alone, this demonstrates that harboring anger serves neither you nor anybody else, for that matter.

Given that this is the situation, you should make a decision to make things better and make a commitment to learning how to let go of your anger and wrath and gradually replace those emotions with tranquillity and peace. Setting a goal that is oriented on improving this aspect of your life and committing yourself to working on it totally until you achieve it is the first step in achieving this. The second stage is to acknowledge that you have a severe issue that requires your attention, investigate it more, understand its signs and symptoms, and develop a goal that is centeredaround improving this aspect of your life.

The steps that need to be taken are as follows.

Acquaint yourself with the Various Forms of Anger

To begin, it is important for you to have an understanding of the many forms of anger so that you can identify the specific kind of anger that you feel. There are primarily three forms of anger: forceful aggression, open aggression, and passive aggression.

1. The Use of Passive Aggression

People who avoid conflict are less likely to confess that they have a difficulty controlling their anger, since they don't want to seem weak. It is probable that you will continue to languish in unhappiness if you steer clear of confrontations and instead bottle up your anger rather than facing it head-on. You are simply fooling yourself despite the fact that you are assuring everyone that "everything is okay" all the time.

Even if you are able to contain your raging rage, you will eventually let it out in some other way, such as by taking it out on random people or situations. You also run the risk of being more prone to lashing out violently at some point in the future, which will only serve to make your difficulties worse in the long run. It is quite possible that you have difficulties with passive aggressive rage if you can identify to this and often find yourself seething alone while pretending that everything is OK while simultaneously hating on everyone else.

2. Unconcealed Aggression

Open aggressiveness, as opposed to passive aggression, entails striking out in anger and being verbally or physically hostile against other people. Your anger is likely to come out in a variety of destructive ways, including things like blackmailing, fighting, arguing, squabbling, backbiting, yelling, accusing, relentlessly criticizing someone, and bullying. The drive to exert control over other people and the circumstances in which they find themselves often lies at the root of overt aggressive behavior. When this need goes unsatisfied, the result might be an angry explosion of words.

You have open aggressive anger if you often shout at other people, whether for a valid or meaningless cause, if you backbite others, if you formulate strategies on how to damage other people, and if you blame others for getting you angry.

Anger that is Used Aggressively

Anger that is directed on oneself and one's environment is the healthiest kind of rage and the correct method for dealing with one's own rage. As was said previously, anger in and of itself is neither a good nor a bad feeling; it is only an emotion; what makes it either positive or negative is your attitude to it.

The correct method to deal with your anger is to first have an understanding of it, then deal with the issue that is driving the anger, then maintain control of your emotions, and last pay attention to the many aspects involved in the scenario so that you may correctly think things through and deal with the circumstance.

You can solve the most difficult problems if you keep a cool head, listen attentively, and speak with self-assurance. This will allow you to convey your side of the argument while being adaptable and receptive to the other side's points of view. The majority of individuals who struggle with anger management difficulties do not communicate their anger in an authoritative manner, which is why they struggle in this area.

Now that you are aware of the three primary categories of anger, you should pay careful attention to your actions and emotions over the next five to ten days in order to determine which category of anger best describes your typical experiences. Because you are reading this book in an effort to find a solution to your anger issue, it is extremely probable that you are someone who typically displays either passive aggression or open aggressiveness when angry.

You may distinguish between the two by determining whether you bottle up your rage or let it all hang out in the open. Having said that, you can also utilize a variety of indications and symptoms to create an accurate self-diagnosis.

You Should Not Underestimate The Risk That Comes With Being Angry.

Even while we are exposed to the most extreme manifestations of anger on a daily basis via the media, there are other, much more covert problems that anger is also responsible for. This kind of fury is known as maladaptive anger, and it's the kind that may lead to someone destroying their own personal belongings, abusing substances, or verbally abusing them over and over again.

Additionally, it causes a broad range of health problems, the first of which is an unnecessary burden placed on the heart. In point of fact, studies have shown that your risk of having a heart attack is increased by a factor of two for a period of two hours following an incident of extreme anger. This does not just refer to instances in which you explode and let your anger out in a manner that is either verbal or violent; keeping your anger suppressed may also contribute to the development of heart disease. This indicates that learning to manage your furious outbursts is a good place to start, but in order to get actual medical advantages from your new lifestyle, you will eventually need to learn how to feel less angry in the first place. Controlling your angry outbursts is a good place to start.

In addition to placing additional pressure on your heart, research has shown that there is a threefold increase in the risk of having a stroke in the two hours after a really furious outburst compared to what it may ordinarily be. Those people who already have an aneurysm waiting in the wings have a risk of stroke that is an astounding six times higher than it would be in any other circumstance.

In addition to this, if you spend the most of your time in an angry mood, you actually damage your immune system. This is because your body will spend more time in a state of flight or fight, which demands greater energy, as opposed to a state of relaxation, in which it can prioritize overall wellbeing. In point of fact, studies have shown that even thinking back to a period when you felt tremendous rage is enough to produce a drop in your antibody levels that may last for as long as six hours.

We are beyond exhausted.

People who are worn out, spent, and nearing the end of their reserves of energy are in the same position as those described above. I have no doubt that everyone has experienced this. You start the day in the office, where you stay for the whole of the day. When you come back, you have some errands to do, and when you finally get home, you have to clean the house and prepare supper. Continue doing this process till the end of the week. At the conclusion of it, you will most likely be an exhausted and irritable mess, and your brain will be unable to focus on anything other than that.

Imagine that when you are in this situation, someone does anything even somewhat annoying or asks you for something. How would you react? They don't have to do anything particularly outrageous; all they have to do is irritate you enough for you to find yourself yelling at them to leave you alone, or even worse, insulting them, before you realize what's happening. It is imperative that you keep in mind that you were not intending any of the negative conduct that you may display towards them. Your energy reserves are at an all-time low, which is the root cause of all the fury that is now manifesting itself.

You have undoubtedly experienced being on the receiving end of someone else's wrath in the past, and you were not aware that it was caused by exhaustion. There are instances when it may be difficult for another person to comprehend. Because of this, we need to give the individuals around us a little bit of leeway. You never know what's going on in someone else's life or the reason why they exploded at you. If it's simply a one-time occurrence, then chalk it up to a bad day and move on. There's no need in dwelling on it.

We are either on the verge of breaking down or completely overloaded.

Have you ever been so preoccupied, anxious, or worn out that you had no idea what you were thinking or how you were feeling? Have you ever been so overtaken by the happenings of your life? I am quite aware that this occurs to me on a regular basis. There are simply moments when I go through extended stretches in which it seems like everything is happening at once, and at such times, I don't have the essential time to think or catch my breath. Everything is such a roller coaster of feelings, and I am always on edge as a result.

When that occurs, it's so simple for me to become furious about the tiniest, most inconsequential things since I'm already in such a bad mood. It's not anything I'm very proud of, but I simply can't take any more pressure at this point. You should be aware that there are moments when you just reach a psychological limit and snap. When that occurs, you have a tendency to take it out on the people around you, which is never a good idea. Or, sometimes, on things that aren't alive at all. Have you ever kicked a chair or a stuffed animal when you were angry or frustrated? Raise your hand if you are guilty of it.

This is fairly comparable to being exhausted or being in an emotional state that is sensitive. It is just more than we are able to deal with, and as a result, we find ourselves losing patience as well as the capacity to think clearly and sensibly. When there is too much going on and the brain is overstimulated, rational cognition goes out the window. You are aware that your computer has the capability of working in overdrive, right? The same may be said for your brain, and the results are not attractive.

The Experience Of Victimization Leads To A Loss Of Agency.

When we convince ourselves that we are the ones who have been wronged and that the events that have transpired were not within our sphere of influence, we will experience a sense of helplessness. If you constantly point the finger at another person when anything bad happens to you, such being late, broke, or irritated, then you are giving that person all of the power. Because of this, you will have the impression that you have no control, which will ultimately lead to deeper problems.

It is a known fact that the majority of the events that occur in our lives are not within our direct control. Simply being born into certain demographics might already place one at a disadvantage. It's possible that you don't have access to as many possibilities as others who have more luxury, but it's important to remember that a lot of things are under our hands, too.

It's possible that you're completely out of money and can't afford to further your education in any way. Because of this, you are unable to acquire a better job and are forced to remain at a location that you despise. Despite the fact that some of these factors may be beyond of your control, the situation as a whole will still determine the outcome. That makes no difference at all. The reality is that you are the only one who can determine whether or not these circumstances will cause you to feel furious.

When responding aggressively to a predicament, one can remark something along the lines of "I can't help it if I'm stressed." Naturally, it's possible that they won't be able to stop themselves from feeling that way even if they try. We each experience a spectrum of feelings, some of which are more difficult to keep under control than others. If a person lets themselves lose their cool in the heat of the moment, they have the ability to completely change the course of events.

The consequences of harboring pent-up rage

In some form or another, every feeling is inevitably going to be communicated. And if a person makes a conscious effort to conceal their wrath, the following are some of the possible outcomes:

It is possible for it to result in a poor mood since the inability to express anger may have a domino effect on other aspects of a person's life, such as how they feel throughout the day. When a person is in a bad mood, it often shows in their relationships with other people.

If the individual is unable to vent their anger to the person who caused it, the aggressiveness does not go away; instead, it will be moved onto something else. This energy may then be diverted to a another item, which can act as their "punching bag" in the process. If you aim this toward strong items, it will be beneficial; but, if you direct it toward delicate objects, animals, or even other humans over whom you have control, it will be destructive. This is because strong objects can better withstand the force.

It is possible for it to have an impact on your health; despite the fact that cortisol and adrenaline are necessary for the "fight or flight" response, it is dangerous for the body to remain in that condition for an extended period of time. It may cause high blood pressure as well as an acceleration of the natural aging process in the body and skin. Not to mention the fact that frowning may speed up the aging process and cause wrinkles to appear on one's face.

By presenting these examples, we have shown the concept of anger as well as the pervasive nature of its presence in our lives. It also explored the probable sources of it, how it manifests itself, and the possible ramifications on the person if it is not voiced.

5. Anger causes anguish for other people

The feeling of anger is infectious, and it quickly becomes widespread. When you're surrounded by unhappy individuals, it's hard to find the joy in life. When one member of a family is upset, the atmosphere in the house might become tense for the other members. If the male in the family isn't content, then the other members of the family won't be able to relax as much. It is impossible to feel at ease in the company of someone who is furious. Anger is contagious, and it has the potential to make one uncomfortable.

6. Being angry might cause you to act in ways that you will always be sorry for.

After their regular argument, a guy went to bed after having a misunderstanding with his wife. The lady was so furious that she went and heated some water, which she then dumped on the guy. The man's yell woke up the residents in the neighborhood. Unfortunately, he passed away as he was being transported to the hospital.

There is no question that this lady will never, ever forget what has just transpired in her life. This deed, which was organized by a single moment of wrath, will continue to hunt her even if God heals her.

7. Being angry might be harmful to your health.

Recurrent, unresolved anger may ultimately cause damage to a wide variety of different bodily systems because it causes a steady rush of stress hormones and the related metabolic changes that go along with that anger. Anger has been related to a variety of health concerns, both short-term and long-term, including the following:

a painful head ache

issues with digestion, such as cramping in the abdomen

the inability to sleep

increased levels of anxiousness

Negative emotions such as sorrow and depression

hypertension; high blood pressure

difficulties with the skin, such as eczema or a heart attack

Anger raises your chance of having a stroke.

Your anger will not help you in any way. Do not make the mistake of quoting Charles Spurgeon when he said, "Do not say, 'I cannot help having a bad temper.'" You really must provide a hand, my friend. Pray to God for immediate assistance in overcoming it, for you either have to kill it yourself or it will kill you. It is impossible to enter the heavenly realm with a foul attitude.

Day 15: Formulate a Strategy

Recognizing the situations that set off your anger is the first step in developing a plan to deal with it. Before you make a strategy, you must first determine the sentiments that lie behind the events that cause you to get angry. This will allow you to effectively combat these emotions whenever you feel them beginning to surface. When you are able to pinpoint the sentiments' origins, you will also be able to identify them in other contexts that are unrelated to the circumstances in which you initially experienced them.

After you have compiled a mental list of the things that set off your anxiety, jot them down on a piece of paper. People often skip this phase because they believe it is not essential to the process. Naturally, you'll keep in mind the circumstances that set off your triggers since they crop up on a daily basis. Having them written down, however, is an essential step in the Anger Plan. Write down your triggers, and then next to them, their underlying reasons. The structure may be something like this: Anger on the road might be defined as the fear of being out of control. It's a really straightforward list, and research shows that straightforwardness helps an incredible amount.

Stick it to the front of the fridge, attach it to the dashboard of your car, or just leave it out on your desk where everyone can see it. Put it in a location where you will see it often during the day. Read it on a daily basis, preferably first thing in the morning before starting your day. Keep in mind that other people do not need to be aware of what it is, but if you feel the need to inform someone else about it, please do so! A highly helpful and effective kind of therapy that can be used in a variety of settings is just having conversations with other people about how you are feeling. You shouldn't let it make you feel ashamed. You have already acknowledged that you have a problem with controlling your anger, and other people will see this as a demonstrable indication of your efforts to improve the situation.

When you look at the list, a lot of different sentiments could come up. All of them are scenarios in which you find yourself on a daily basis or virtually on a daily basis, and all of them are scenarios in which you are aware that you behave in a manner that is harmful to both yourself and the people around you. It could be challenging to put it in writing, and it might be much more challenging to display it publicly. You could have feelings of embarrassment, despair, or possibly even greater rage. It is never pleasant to be reminded of one's flaws, and ineffective control of one's anger might be considered to be one of those flaws. Keep in mind that the list is not a kind of self-inflicted punishment. It is a constructive activity that benefits you in a variety of different ways! This is just another stage of the anger management plan.

Not only does the list serve to remind you every day of the things that need your attention, but it also acts as a daily reminder of the things that you have already achieved. It is critical that we often bring to our own attention the things that we have previously accomplished. When we are feeling unmotivated or as if we have gone off the wagon with our anger management, it might act as a source of inspiration for us. Simply because you already have the list in your possession, you have successfully completed a number of the necessary procedures. When you start to experience bad emotions, it's helpful to be able to bring this positive thought back to mind.

Now you have a list of the triggers and an understanding of their root causes. The creation of a response guide that details each step in sequential order is the next phase. You need to have a precise plan for when your anger hits, and the quickest way to get this done is to break the process down into phases. When your anger strikes, you need to have a clear plan. Make a strategy and write it down for the next time you feel road rage. For instance, your plan may be to "take three deep breaths and count to 5." Whatever it is, there is no pressing need to go into great detail about it. It is essentially simply a list of the methods that you will use in order to assist you in controlling your anger. It could be helpful to have this plan with you at all times or to read it before beginning each new day. If you put in the necessary amount of effort and practice, it will ultimately become natural to you.

Learn How To Settle Your Nerves.

As soon as you become aware that you are becoming angry, regardless of how large or how little the cause may be, you need to immediately begin working on calming yourself down and getting rid of your anger. This is not an easy effort, but if you can identify the precise time when you realize you are furious and can somehow move it into your controls, then you will be able to learn how to manage your anger intelligently. This is not an easy task.

Later on, in the next chapter, we will go over several techniques in more depth to help you relax.

Rule No. 3: Stay away from what sets you off.

An action or a statement, for example, might be a trigger that causes anger in anybody, and everyone has these triggers. Take, for instance, the fact that you are a laid-back person who prefers to approach life at a more leisurely pace than most people do. Obviously, not everyone acknowledges or comprehends the significance of this. What do you get? You can get labels like "lazy" or "idle," which are descriptors that drive you absolutely crazy.

Consider, instead, that you have a strong aversion to smoking, and the very thought of somebody smoking around you causes you to feel an unreasonable amount of rage. Whether you're at a party or a restaurant, if you look around and see other people smoking around you, you can always predict whether or not you're going to become irritated and lash out.

These two ideas, smoking and the thought of being termed "lazy" or "idle," are the things that set off your triggers. You'll be able to maintain control of your fury if you only steer clear of these potential flashpoints. This may require very little effort on your part, but the benefits will be well worth the effort.

Stay away from those who think you are unproductive or lazy. If you see any talk moving in that direction, you should withdraw your participation and leave the room. Steer clear of the subject, and stay away from talks that will inevitably circle back to your routines. Stay away from restaurants, bars, and other public areas where smoking is allowed. Put up signs warning people not to smoke at your place of business, your vehicle, and your house. If someone you're talking to is going to light up, you should gently tell them that you don't enjoy the scent and then quit the discussion.

If there are some individuals who you do not get along with, or those who, as the proverb goes, "just rub you the wrong way," it is best to steer clear of them. If you run into them at a social event or a business function, all you need to do is say "hello" and "goodbye" and then go on with your day. Don't give such people the opportunity to get you worked up.

Alterations To One's Way Of Life May Help In Anger Management.

Dealing with your anger in the near term should go hand in hand with developing more long-term strategies for anger management. Because of this, certain modifications to one's conduct and maybe some enhancements to one's quality of life are required. The following is a list of the items that are highly suggested for you to attempt.

Try to be less resistant to the current state of affairs. Our inability to accept things in their current state is a significant contributor to the irritation we feel. People who have the perception that their lives are not unfolding as they should are more likely to experience this. The reality is that nothing ever changes, and you can only work with what you have. It is true that we constantly work toward achieving the finest possible outcomes, but after those outcomes have been achieved, we must focus on maximizing their potential.

Put an end to your unhealthy attachment to the way things ought to be. Not only is it a beneficial frame of mind, but so is contentment—provided it is practiced at the appropriate moment. acquire rid of the mindset that says "all or nothing" since it's more probable that you'll end up with nothing than that you'll ever acquire everything. You will only make a terrible impression on others if you show anger because someone only gave you 90% of what you asked for.

Try to be more lenient. You need to master the art of letting go, even if the advice seems corny or overused. Put an end to ruminating on things that have already transpired in the past. Even if you were well within your rights to be furious about what your buddy did to you, you do not have the right to feel angry about it now or, for that matter, for the rest of your life. In point of fact, it is best if you let go of things as soon as they are finished (that is, when you can no longer change the outcome of the situation). Do you remember what they said about lamenting over milk that has already been spilled? It is a far more serious problem when it causes you to get irritated.

Have some fun with it. Within the realm of interpersonal communication, humor is a tremendously potent instrument. When things are going badly, it's a fantastic way to break the uncomfortable vibe that's been building up. Laughter, in addition to its physiological benefits, has been shown to have a contagious quality that may lift the spirits of others and flip frowns upside down. When everything has gone to hell in a handbasket, the only thing left to do is laugh at the situation. It's definitely preferable than getting angry about it, that much can be said for sure.

Imagine just the best. Always try to look at things as if the glass were half full rather than half empty. The most successful businesspeople will tell you that even in the most difficult circumstances, there are chances to make the most of what you have. The greatest part is that this isn't something that just applies in the corporate world. At first, circumstances could make you angry, but choosing to focus on the positive aspects of the situation might help you earn something in return.

Be careful not to become too attached. There are times when the only thing that can set you off on a rage-filled path is yourself. People have a tendency to get too interested in activities that they may not even be a part of anyhow. This occurs all too often. This is relevant in a wide variety of contexts, including the following:

An excessive amount of labor. Make time for yourself, already! Putting yourself in a stressful situation won't do anything except make you more inclined to lose your cool.

allowing yourself to get emotionally invested in a dispute that was not your responsibility in the first place. This does not imply that you should have a callous attitude toward the struggles of other people. You have a responsibility to look out for yourself as well, or else you can wind up need even more assistance than your buddy, who is already in such a precarious situation.

allowing oneself to be affected by the news. There is no question that awful things are occurring all around the globe. You really shouldn't let it spoil your day, especially if you don't have a solution for the conflicts that are going on in other countries. You should just accept the things you see on TV at face value and make an effort to avoid jumping on the anxious bandwagon of internet haters.

Take some action! Always make sure you're giving your body a decent exercise! It's the greatest approach to make sure you don't have any extra energy that may perhaps be channeled into anger later on. Always make time to play, since this is the period during which you will never be furious (unless, of course, you are a five-year-old who happens to be a spoiled loser).

Take into consideration the fact that you also have the option of engaging in hobbies like yoga that help relieve tension.

People who struggle to effectively regulate their anger are often considered to be unhealthy. Therefore, it should come as no surprise that the greatest answer is to adopt a way of life that is good not just physically but also emotionally and psychologically! Have a life that will make you more upbeat, charitable, and content with yourself.

Talking therapy

The following are some signs that an individual may need the intervention of a professional or medical personnel:

• Finding oneself in legal hot water

• Frequently reporting that they are required to stifle their fury

• Engaging in intense arguments on a regular basis with members of one's family, acquaintances, or colleagues

- Taking part in fights or other violent altercations in public

- Physically abusing one's partner or one's kid

- Making violent threats against other people or their property

- Caused damage to nearby structures as a consequence of the volcanic eruption

- Losing their temper while driving and acting in an unpredictable manner

Anger issues almost seldom occur in isolation. They may be brought on by a wide range of distinct mental health problems, including the following:

• Dependence on alcoholic beverages or illicit narcotics

• A disorder known as bipolar

• Personality disorders characterized by schizophyte features

• Disorders of psychosis

• A personality condition that is dangerously close to collapsing

It's possible that treating the underlying reasons of wrath is all that's needed to bring down the intensity of those feelings. On the other hand, there are times when an individual has to learn to control their wrath on their own terms.

Management therapy may take the form of meetings with a counselor or therapist on an individual basis, or it may take the form of group sessions.

If a person has been diagnosed with a mental health issue, such as depression, anger management should be a consideration in their treatment plan.

Training in anger control teaches one how to, among other things:

- Be aware of the possible triggering events

- Respond in a productive manner, whether in the throes of anger or in advance of the situation

- Recognize and address the causal factors.

- Train irrational and excessive cognitive tendencies to be more rational

- Restore an attitude of serenity and composure to yourself.

- In situations that are likely to provoke anger and frustration, it is important to convey feelings and needs in a manner that is direct but not aggressive.

- Commit more time and resources to finding solutions to problems.

With the assistance of a therapist or counselor, you may be able to get answers to the following questions:

- How can I know if I'm becoming upset with myself?

- What sorts of people, situations, events, and places, in addition to other forms of triggers, bother me the most?

- When I'm furious, what should I do with myself? So, what should I do at this point?

• How does my anger affect others who are in the same room with me?

It may be good to acknowledge that wrath and calmness are not sensations that are mutually exclusive to one another. For instance, one's level of fury might range from mild irritation to full-blown rage.

Individuals who have a better understanding of the spectrum may be better able to differentiate between the times when they are really angry and the times when they are just overreacting to little annoyances. One of the primary purposes of therapy is to provide assistance to patients in identifying and responding appropriately to these disparities.

Figure Out How To Keep Yourself In Check.

The first step in effectively controlling your feelings is to become aware of and consciously control your emotional responses. When you experience feelings that are too much for you to handle, this is due to the fact that the rational half of your brain is being overridden by the emotional reaction. It will be difficult for you to digest information if you are currently going through an episode of emotional hijacking.

Our amygdala experiences high levels of activation while we are operating in settings that are high in stress. It isn't always simple to grasp what we're feeling and why we're feeling that way. It's also not always easy to explain our feelings to others. Because of this, it is essential for everyone of us to maintain a level of awareness of our own selves. The following are some strategies that can assist you in managing your emotions and thinking more clearly.

Take a few deep breaths and relax.

The simple act of pausing for a moment to take a breath may work wonders for us at times. When our minds aren't functioning correctly, we often lose control of our breathing. It is possible to become more aware of the here-and-now by pausing briefly and then taking several deep breaths. You start to have a heightened awareness of both yourself and the world around you.

Try taking a few deep breaths whenever you feel as if your emotions are getting the better of you. This helps you to disconnect from your thoughts and reconnect with your body. Your amygdala will take control of your responses if you do not take a few deep breaths at that precise instant. The reasoning area of your brain, known as the prefrontal cortex, becomes more active as your state of calm improves.

Recognize and accept your feelings.

It is critical that we have a solid grasp on our feelings. It assists us in gaining a better understanding of what it is that we need, what it is that we desire, and what it is that we do not want. When we have a better understanding of our feelings, we are better able to communicate those sentiments, we are better able to manage disagreements, and we are able to get through difficult feelings more quickly.

Put off the topic for a while.

It's possible that you won't always be able to keep your emotions under control in some circumstances. If you are having a discussion with someone who is causing you to have intense feelings at the time, it is best to take a minute to compose yourself, take a deep breath, and remind yourself that you can always postpone the talk rather than responding rashly. When you purposefully delay your answer, you also give the other person time to gather their thoughts and respond appropriately. If you do this, you save yourself from saying anything that you could, at a later time, come to regret.

A Calm State Can Easily Be Maintained If You Follow These Easy Steps

Here are some particular actions that you may perform on a daily basis in order to further assist you in the important duty of preserving your calm condition.

You should make it a habit to conduct your breathing exercises first thing in the morning, as soon as you open your eyes.

You have the option of following the stages in chapter 5 that came before, or you may take the actions that are listed below. You should be standing tall on your feet, with your back also straight, and your arms outstretched in front of you. While you elevate your body up on your toes, take a long, deep breath in through your nose. Hold for a total of six seconds. Force yourself to exhale through your lips as you bring your torso and your toes closer together. Carry out these processes a minimum of ten to twenty times.

Imagine going through the day calm and collected rather than anxious and irritable.

Imagine going about your day in a relaxed manner, doing all of the tasks that are required of you. You are able to recognize, on some level, that you do not feel stressed out and that you are, in fact, calm. Always remember to do this first thing in the morning, before you go out to work or get started on your housework. Maintain the picture in your head for the whole of the day.

Make it a point to be calm and collected even while you're hard at work.

Perform the breathing exercises whenever you notice that you are becoming frustrated or agitated while you are at work. You are free to carry it out in any setting and any posture. When you are dealing with the public, you have the opportunity to be more understated about it. You are free to do this action either standing or sitting, with or without closing your eyes. That is one of the benefits of doing breathing exercises. They are there whenever they are needed.

Make sure that you are able to keep up this level of calmness throughout the whole day.

You will be able to achieve this goal if you make it a habit to meditate or do your breathing exercises whenever you feel the beginnings of tension accumulating inside of you. Don't wait for it to reach its peak before taking action. If you don't deal with these potential sources of tension right once, they could build up to the point where they become overwhelming. Make sure they understand who the boss is.

Reflect on the events that have transpired over the day.

Conduct an analysis to determine whether or not you were successful in achieving your objective of preserving your level of composure. You should make a note of the situations in which you discover that you were unable to do anything, then focus on improving your performance the next time you are faced with a similar challenge.

5.) Resist the Urge to Discipline Your Child in the Heat of the Moment: You should make it a priority to avoid correcting your children while you are feeling furious. Any effort you make to punish your kid in the evening will result in sending the incorrect message to him in the long run.

Discipline should never originate from a position of pain and fury, but rather from a place of empathy and love for the child being disciplined.

Also, in the process of enforcing discipline, you should avoid using any kind of physical force on the kid, such as punching or slapping them.

It's possible that spanking your kid may make you feel better in the moment because it will allow you to let out some of the anger that's been building up, but it's not good for your child's development as a whole.

6.) Watch Your Tone, Be Careful With Your Word Choice, and Stay Away From Threats:

The sharing of feelings is analogous to making a deal. What you put into anything is precisely what you get back. Research has shown that when we communicate to other people in a calm manner, not only do we feel more calm ourselves, but also the other person is more likely to reply to us in a calm manner.

In a similar manner, when we raise our voices, curse at, or threaten other people, it causes them to feel defensive and dish out the same kind of behaviorin response, which makes the situation much worse. This is also true about the connection you have with your children.

7.) Make A List Of Possible Ways To Handle Situations: When things are peaceful at home, call your kids together and speak to them. When things are calm at home, call your kids together and talk to them. Talk to them about the things you anticipate from them. Discuss the several methods in which you may all deal with and express your anger. Discuss the part that each member of the household plays in ensuring that it is a warm, caring, and secure place to live.

8.) Choose How You Would Like To Respond: I want you to take notice of this: Every argument or disagreement you have with your children depletes the priceless relationship capital you have accumulated in their emotional bank account with you.

Your connection with them will suffer greater harm the more you nag, shout, and scream at them, slap them, and threaten them.

Choose the things to which you react and the things to which you do not respond in order to avoid using positive emotional capital that you have with them that is not necessary. It may be in your best interest to ignore part of their behavior rather than respond furiously to it. This is especially true in certain situations.

Keep in mind that the more engaged and beneficial your connection is with your children, the greater the likelihood is that they will respect you. And to the extent that people respect you, the more likely they are to comply with the directions you provide.

Meditation: Don't Take It Personally

The following is a practice that will help you become better at not taking other people's comments or criticisms personally. As a method, we will be using a mantra that is more relevant to present times. Throughout the course of the day, keep an eye out for instances in which you feel the beginnings of anger rising inside you, particularly when it comes to relatively little matters. For example, you take that jar of pickles out of the refrigerator, and you work as hard as you can to screw off the lid so that you can get your hands on a pickle because you want one so much. You exert a lot of effort, yet there is still no pickle. Try telling yourself either out loud or to yourself in your head: "It's not personal." Take a few deep breaths, and if it helps, repeat the phrase to yourself once more. After that, you'll be able to go back to work on the pickle jar. You run it under hot water, you wipe the lid dry, and you give it your best grip, but it still won't budge. Despite your best efforts, it just won't move. Pickles are pretty about the only thing left on earth that can bring a smile to your face at this point. Take a minute to calm yourself and keep telling yourself, "It's not personal." Repeat it a few more times while paying attention to your breathing.

This exercise will perhaps help you get a fresh perspective on some of the cognitive biases that contribute to anger and make the situation a great deal worse. For instance, you could believe that this pickle firm has something personal against you. I have never been successful in opening pickle jars. I am reviled by pickles. Everyone in the world is working against me. Observe how there is less for anger to latch onto when these personally tailored distortions are removed from the equation. This practice may also be used on situations that are more difficult and may evoke strong emotions.

Fury in One's Residence

Anger in the family that is not properly controlled can be so devastating over time that many of the world's faiths have been trying to figure out how to deal with it for millennia. The maintenance of tranquility inside one's own four walls is seen as very important in Jewish tradition. The name given to this teaching is Shalom Bayit. There is a teaching in the Talmud that states, "If one brings peace into the home, it is as though peace were brought to all of the people of Israel." The Buddhist teaching of loving-kindness, the numerous Christian teachings linked to loving thy neighbor, and other comparable teachings may be found across the world's many spiritual and religious traditions. This idea has a striking connection to all of these concepts.

Anger that is not properly handled may result in the destruction of fundamental relationships, including those between parents and children, as well as between siblings. It is even capable of taking extended families and splintering them, sometimes with no way to resolve the conflict. This may vary from family members retaining grudges and resentments that lead to a lifetime of not talking to one another to arguments over who gets to keep the remote control or who is the favorite kid. This can also include fights over trivial matters such as who gets the remote control or who is the favorite child. When it comes to the short, medium, and long-term development of abilities for anger control, all of these are our primary concerns. We want to take care of previously ingrained resentments and grudges so that we may have a more pleasant internal and external existence with people who are closest to us. We also want to deal with the minor things for its own sake and so that it doesn't evolve into the large stuff.

Maintaining the most important aspect

In any event, the sorrow is misguided when it is only recognized and experienced as complaints and blames in others instead of what one may term one's own defenselessness. The individual suffering and the damage done to relationships by protective fury is pretty evident. This leads to never-ending efforts, which are often fruitless, to alter other people or to bolster one's own tendency toward force by examining and rejecting the beliefs and actions of others. It is an inadequate struggle, which only leads to pain since it does not address the actual suffering that is being endured.

It may be helpful to discuss your situation with a guide, therapist, or trusted friend in order to address the hidden issues of powerlessness that may be driving these responses if you come to the realization that some of your quick and strong or constant furious reactions might actually be concealing tension. If you come to this realization, it may be helpful to talk about your situation.

How would you describe the role that rage plays in your life now that you're an adult? Do you resort to rage in order to exert control and persuade other people to comply with your demands? Do you try to manage other people by being agreeable in the hopes that this would prevent them from being angry with you? When people are angry, do you shut down, retreat, and reject them in order to rebuff them and ensure that you are not ruled by them?

Anger, accusations, feedback, and judgment are all strategies that may be used in an effort to exert control over other people. Being agreeable and excellent are other strategies that may be used to affect how other people feel about you and how they behave toward you.

Both putting up a fight and pulling away are covert strategies that may be used to exert influence on other people while maintaining one's own autonomy. Every one of these behaviors creates dominating hierarchies, which do not function well in any kind of relationship.

Controlling techniques, on the other hand, render concordance and intimacy impossible rather than really producing them.

The Effects That Feeling Angry Has On Our Children

Anger of a certain degree is acceptable and even natural; but, the effects of furious parenting may be very damaging to children. These repercussions might be apparent in the manner in which they interact with other youngsters. The repercussions will have further effects. The experiences we have as children have the potential to shape who we become as adults and, in certain cases, to be handed down from one generation to the next.

The following are some of the consequences of furious parenting:

The child is less empathetic toward others; the child has difficulty adjusting to change; the child can experience serious mental health issues; the child may abuse their spouse or their own children; the child may have limited career and financial achievement; the child is more likely to be delinquent.

The results of furious parenting may have very negative effects on children. You are blessed with the capacity to exert control over your emotions. Even though it could be a lengthy path that's littered with obstacles along the way, it's important to try to fix the problem as soon as possible since doing so is more likely to be successful.

Understanding your feelings of rage is the first step in learning how to control them. In most cases, the anger that exists between parents and children is at least somewhat unreasonable. Psychologists have a term for this phenomenon; they call it "the ghost in the nursery." When a kid is distressed, a parent may unconsciously recall their own experiences and fears that they had as a child. This phenomena indicates that this occurs when a child is upset. After then, the parent responds in the same way that they did when they were confronted with the situation for the first time. This happens on an unconscious level, so the parent is completely unaware that any of this is going place. On the other hand, revisiting the worries they had as children is really overpowering, which is why it is understandable that the parents are reacting irrationally.

To one's own detriment

Anger that is difficult to manage and is negative might lead to self-destruction. When you are often furious, you have a greater propensity to feel the need to respond to everything, whether vocally, non-verbally, or violently. Because being furious, yelling, having an outburst, or even becoming violent affects not only your body but also your mind, psychology, and emotions, these behaviors are all warning signs that you are heading down the road to self-destruction. When you're angry, you lose contact with both yourself and the world around you. If you are unable to exercise self-control over your anger, you may find that you engage in behaviors that, under normal circumstances, you would avoid. These behaviors, however, may have consequences that are detrimental to your mental and psychological health. For instance, a person who lashes out at a loved one in a fit of irrational wrath may come to deeply regret their actions, and they may find it impossible to forgive themselves.

Problems with one's health

One of the many reasons why anger is harmful and destructive is the fact that it may cause us to have health problems. Research has shown that persons who often experience negative emotions, such as anger and fury, are more likely to have a higher degree of health risks than those who seldom experience these emotions. An abnormally elevated heart rate might be the result of being angry. This indicates that when you get upset, your heart starts to beat faster than usual, and because of this, an increased pulse rate above normal acts as a trigger for heart attacks. Also, displaying anger on a regular basis may leave a person feeling exhausted after their outbursts, which can lead to stress, which can lead to major psychological and physiological difficulties such as cardiovascular disease, depression, high blood pressure, and a great deal of other conditions.

The inability to get quality sleep is yet another negative effect that rage has on one's health. Anger causes a rise in the levels of both adrenaline and noradrenaline in the body, and since these chemicals are constantly racing through your system, you will have trouble falling or staying asleep as a result of your state of anger. If you don't already know what lack of sleep can do to the human body, you should know that it can impair your mental alertness and make your body more susceptible to a variety of illnesses. If you don't already know what lack of sleep can do to the human body, you should know what it can do. One of the many reasons why you should try to control your anger is because it may have a negative impact on your physical health and is one of the reasons why anger is generally unhealthy for a person.

Insufficiency in Sleep

Problems with controlling one's anger may lead to sleep deprivation, and this is particularly true when there is an underlying problem with one's emotional, physical, or mental health that is the cause of the anger. Studies, such as those that were published in the Journal of Experimental Psychology: General, have connected a lack of sleep to individuals being a lot faster to anger. This may lead to challenges with anger management, since sleep deprivation can also contribute to issues with anger management. Anyone who has ever gone more than two days without sleep is well aware of how bad they feel; their responses become sluggish, their focus becomes as cloudy as Swiss cheese, and their levels of annoyance begin to climb. Even the most level-headed individual is capable of transforming into Mr. Hyde when they are sleep deprived, and those who already struggle with anger management may find that they are pushed far over the red line and completely lose control of their emotions as a result.

Concern or worry

People who suffer from anxiety are often either chronic worriers or people-pleasers. They have a tendency to be too critical of themselves, despite the fact that others see them as being courteous, nice, and even timid. Overachievers, or those that society has a tendency to label as nerds, tend to give off an impression of being responsible and diligent. Additionally, they are often fairly nice and compassionate individuals who may also be introverted. An outpouring of rage from them is the one thing that nobody could ever anticipate happening. Anxiety, on the other hand, may be a veritable powder keg for rage, and the adage "still waters run deep" perfectly represents the majority of individuals who struggle with this condition. In addition to this, these individuals have a pattern of stuffing their feelings, despite the fact that the human body has a finite capacity for repression until it breaks. According to a research conducted by Concordia University, anger may actually make a person's anxiety symptoms worse. Although the majority of people who suffer from anxiety will keep their feelings to themselves, there is always the possibility that a seemingly little event might trigger a full-blown panic attack.

People who have problems controlling their anger may discover that it is simpler for them to retreat from the social activities of day-to-day life. What they formerly found to be relaxing and enjoyable may suddenly seem like a chore because they have to contend with a variety of irritants that have the potential to set them off. The majority of the time, removing yourself from a situation that has left you feeling wounded, deceived, and furious enables you to better deal with the emotions you are experiencing rather than losing your cool. When a person has been through emotional trauma, they may begin to have panic attacks, which may then lead to bouts of annoyance, which can stoke the fires of an angry state of mind. When a person has been angry for a long time, they may become irrational and violent. They find that remaining away from other people and maintaining their own carefully kept environment gives them the most peace of mind. This is the way they prefer it, and it becomes their home. A location in which they do not have to worry about losing their temper or being irritated with the people and the environment around them since they are free to just be themselves in this setting.

When you are upset, it might seem as if your behavior, ideas, and words are no longer in line with reality.

When you are at your most enraged, you are likely to say or do things that aren't desired because you aren't thinking about the effect it will have on other people, you are likely to act on impulse without thinking about the implications of your actions, and you are only able to think about the negative things that have occurred to you without even giving the positive a second thought.

Your fury will always win, even if your reason is telling you that what you are doing is in no way in line with the standards and values that you hold dear.

When it appears as if rationality has deserted you, the next best thing to do is relax—something you have already learned how to do in the chapter before this one. On the other hand, this is just the beginning of anger control.

When you have already succeeded in calming down and in ridding your mind of any negative ideas, you are now prepared to go on to the fourth phase of anger management, which is to examine the circumstances.

Determine the source of your anger by thinking back on the event from earlier in the day that made you angry and reflecting on how it made you feel. Why do you believe it was that the person who struck you in the face caused you to get furious at them?

When you were upset, was it because you were physically harmed, or because you felt as if you had been betrayed?

It will be easier for you to get over your anger if you examine the circumstances around it and identify the things that contributed to your thoughts, feelings, and behaviors at the time.

If you become furious because you were physically harmed, you should reassure yourself that the injuries you sustained were not serious enough to need medical attention. You might also reassure yourself that the discomfort will go at some point.

If, on the other hand, you believe that the latter was the cause of your anger, then there may have been a more profound significance to what happened that you are not aware of.

It's possible that an egotistical attitude or anything that occurred to you in the past is to blame for the feeling that you've been deceived.

It is possible that you will need to do an introspective analysis of yourself, your previous experiences, and your views in relation to this matter.

Do you find yourself becoming too angry?

There are psychological tests that may determine your amount of fury, your vulnerability to rage, and your level of ability to control your wrath.

If you do battle with anger, though, there is a strong probability that you already know this about yourself.

If you find that you are behaving in ways that are scary or out of control, you may need support in learning how to use coping methods that are more successful.

Why Some People Become More Angry Than Others And What Causes It.

Some individuals have what's known as a "hot head," which means they become furious more rapidly and powerfully than the typical person does. Other people, on the other hand, are perpetually irritated and grouchy even if they don't show their anger in outwardly dramatic ways.

People who are easily offended may not necessarily yell and hurl things; rather, they may withdraw socially, mope about, or get physically unwell as a result of their sensitivity.

People who are quickly agitated often have what some psychologists call a poor tolerance for irritation. This simply means that they feel they shouldn't have to go through anything frustrating, inconvenient, or annoying in their lives.

They are unable to accept things for what they are and get particularly irate if anything seems unjust, such as when they are scolded for a little mistake. They are unable to accept things for what they are.

What accounts for the actions of these individuals?

a great number of things.

There may be genetic or physiological factors at play here:

There is evidence that certain children are born irritable, sensitive, and quickly agitated, and that these symptoms begin to show up at a very early age. This is also true for the age at which these characteristics first appear.

Diversity in sociocultural practices might be another.

We are commonly taught that it is OK to express other emotions, such as worry or despair, but that it is not acceptable to express anger since it is perceived as having a negative connotation.

Because of this, we never learn how to exercise control over it or put it to productive use.

According to the findings of study, a person's family history is significant.

People who are quick to take offense generally come from homes that are disorganized, argumentative, and lacking in emotional intelligence.

Is it OK to "let it all hang out"?

According to the findings of modern psychologists, this is a very harmful misconception.

This argument is used as justification for harming other people by some individuals.

According to the findings of the study, the strategy of "letting it rip" will not assist in resolving the issue for either you or the person with whom you are upset. Your hostility and fury will only increase as a result of this action.

Finding out what it is that sets you off is the most important step you can take before developing a strategy to stop those things that set you off from driving yourself over the edge.

Put yourself in the position of the other person.

It is essential to have the ability to empathize with the other person, which means being able to put yourself in her shoes. When individuals are disturbed, they want us to fully comprehend the reasons for their agitation; they want us to be able to see things from their point of view. Consider what it would be like to be in the other person's shoes for a moment.

Keep an open mind and heart while you listen.

It is important to be open to the possibility that you can learn something about yourself or your way of behaving from the feedback you are receiving or that you may be able to look at a situation from a different perspective, even though it is not necessary to change your views in order to be a good listener. It is possible to acquire new knowledge from every person you converse with.

Figure Out How To Have A Just Fight

We are unable to avoid confrontation. It is an essential component of any kind of connection, but particularly of romantic ones. The more helpless you are and the more reliant you are on another person, the more power that person has to harm you, and as a result, the more power they have to anger you. The ability of two people in a relationship to find healthy ways to communicate their frustrations with one another and find resolutions to those frustrations is critical to the partnership's long-term viability. It is a sign of a strong and healthy relationship when both parties are able to feel comfortable expressing their anger to one another. When one or both participants in a relationship are unwilling to accept their own anger or listen to the rage of their partner, the relationship is more likely to be fragile and stilted rather than robust and spontaneous. It's possible that neither spouse is certain that their relationship can survive the other person letting their emotions out.

Establish ground rules that both you and the other person can live by, and stop being afraid of rage. This will assist you in starting out on an even psychological basis. You are free to come up with your own ground rules, but I would recommend include the following fundamental assumptions in them: we shall take turns listening to one another.

We shall treat each other with courtesy and respect regardless of where we stand.

We are aware that everyone is entitled to his or her own opinion, sentiments, and stance, and we respect that.

We are going to make every effort to locate a remedy for our predicament and an explanation for the cause of our rage.

We have come to the conclusion that there will be no pointing fingers, insults, personal assaults, low blows, threats, or intimidation.

There will be no manipulation, deceptive schemes, or exploitative methods used.

There is never an acceptable reason to resort to striking, shoving, or any other type of abusive behavior.

Setting Up A Just Fight Schedule

You should make it a priority to speak to the person you have a problem with as soon as you can. Your talk will be more fruitful if it lasts for a shorter amount of time. On the other hand, the matter becomes more complicated when there is a longer delay between when someone is upset and when they convey their feelings to the other person. On the other side, you should allow some time for yourself to calm down before approaching your spouse. Make sure that you both have time set apart when you won't be disturbed or interrupted while you're trying to have a conversation. You will learn to fight more successfully and equitably if you follow these suggestions:

While under the influence of drugs or alcohol, do not dispute.

Check to see that you aren't arguing about something you don't understand.

Focus on resolving one problem at a time.

Describe how the situation makes you feel or the sensations it causes you.

It is impolite to tell another individual what you think or feel about them.

Remain focused on the here and now and steer clear of bringing up difficulties from the past.

When the pressure begins to get to you, step back and take a break.

You should strive to come up with a workable solution or compromise, but you should also allow space for "agreeing to disagree."

You shouldn't let your disagreement go on and on like this. In the next half an hour, you should make an effort to get everything under control, at least temporarily.

Make a promise to finish what you start. If you are unable to find a solution to a significant problem, you should seek therapy.

Defining The Different Stages Of Development

When talking about the several phases that a kid goes through throughout their development, it is almost hard to identify the exact moments when they go on to the next stage. The reality is that children will go from one stage to the next at their own individual pace. The majority of the time, each youngster moves to the beat of their own drum. Therefore, we cannot anticipate that every kid will transfer at the same time.

When attempting to define the phases of growth, we need to consider the bigger picture. The primary contours of a child's development may be shown using these broad strokes of the brush. To this extent, children across the board are equivalent to one another. The particulars of a child's personality are what set them apart from all other children in the world.

Please keep in mind that the growth of a kid is influenced by a variety of circumstances. These aspects include a person's familial and social life, as well as the place in which they live and the education they get. Even while we can't generalize, we may make the assumption that some circumstances have a greater impact on children than others.

Take a look at the following scenario:

In general, children who are raised in homes that are loving tend to have higher levels of self-confidence than children who are raised in homes that are abusive. This illustration demonstrates how crucial the environment a kid grows up in is to their entire growth and development.

Jean Piaget, a renowned Swiss psychologist, is credited with being the first person to postulate the existence of phases in the development of children. He felt that children go through four distinct phases on their way to becoming adults. Piaget's discoveries allowed current psychologists to advance their knowledge and comprehension of children's maturation to a greater extent than they could have done so without him.

Piaget's primary research interest was on the cognitive growth of children, which is an important point to emphasize. To put it another way, he was mainly concerned with the growth of the mind and the emotions. Piaget's study was not primarily concerned with how the body develops. Nevertheless, he did emphasize the need of adequate physical development in order to guarantee healthy cognitive progress.[18]

Piaget was the first person to split the development of children into four basic stages:

Birth through two years is the sensorimotor stage.

Two to seven years are required for the preoperational phase, whereas seven to eleven years are required for the operational phase.

Formal operating requirements include being at least 12 years old.

There are cognitive and physical milestones associated with each stage. As a consequence of this, a child's physical development and mental development must occur simultaneously for the child's overall development to be complete in each phase. So, with that in mind, why don't we take a closer look at each stage?

Revealing Your Own Personal Manner Of Anger

Do not allow yourself to be easily angered in your soul, because it is in the lap of fools that rage rests.

- Chapter 7:9 of Ecclesiastes

Everyone's angry outbursts, how their anger builds up, and the window of time that exists between the two are unique to them, as are the manner in which they express their wrath.

For some individuals, a trigger is something that causes them to rapidly respond. Others, on the other hand, spend a considerable amount of time to collect themselves before responding physically or verbally to the cause of their fury. In the second scenario, the person's rage develops gradually over time, leading to an explosive conclusion.

Finding out how you express anger can help you become more aware of the triggers that set off your anger in the first place.

When someone first begins to feel furious, most of the time they are completely unaware of it. You don't typically become aware of it until the physical manifestations of anger (such as heart palpitations, a constriction of the chest, raised blood pressure, headaches, and adrenaline racing through your veins) make themselves known to you.

The manifestations of anger are just the surface of the emotion. Before it develops into anger, it could begin as anything simple, such a notion or a sensation of annoyance.

According to the findings of a research that was carried out by the Harvard Medical School, around 8% of teenagers exhibit anger problems that are sufficient to warrant a lifelong diagnosis of the intermittent explosive disorder.

There are many distinct manifestations or categories of rage, including the following:

ANGER THAT IS AGGRESSIVE

"In an effort to look taller, some people choose to lop off the heads of others." — Yogananda, Paramhansa

When things do not go according to the person's predetermined course of action, the individual with aggressive rage feels the need to control the scene around him as well as his own circumstances, which ends up leading in an eruption of violence.

You want everything to go according to your plan, and you use anger to coerce other people into giving in to your demands.

In order to achieve what you want, you resort to a variety of tactics including humiliation, put-downs, complaints, threats, and abusive language.

This may result in negative consequences, such as a painful confrontation, tarnished reputations, and broken relationships.

ANGER THAT IS ASSERTIVE

An person may be said to be expressing his anger in a constructive manner when he does so in a way that will lead to change and assist in the fulfillment of his needs and goals, but does so without causing grief or devastation to others. They do not wait for people to read their minds and instead communicate their requirements in an open and forthright manner.

It is important to be able to communicate your anger clearly while avoiding trampling on the rights and limits of other people while doing so.

ANXIETY THAT IS ONGOING

This is a persistent feeling of anger against other people, circumstances, and even oneself. An people who struggles with chronic anger has probably been badly injured, and the pain has likely had a lasting impact on his or her life, making it seem to be difficult to move on. Because it lasts for such a long time, this fury is harmful to the individual's health.

ANGER THAT IS VOLATILE

When you're experiencing this kind of rage, you tend to act rashly and get worked up about the smallest of annoyances as well as the most significant of them. Because it appears out of nowhere, it gives others the impression that they need to tread carefully around you in order to avoid offending you. It is very harmful, and as a result, many relationships have been severed as a result.

ANGER THAT IS PASSIVE-AGGRESSIVE

This sort of rage is defined by a persistent avoidance of confrontation, suppression, and denial of the sentiments of anger and frustration that you are now experiencing. It is also characterized by an inability to express anger.

The emotions are communicated in a subtle manner via actions and behaviors such as sarcasm, the silent treatment, withholding love and affection, gossiping, and refusing to collaborate.

They also engage in behaviors that are detrimental to their own success, such as persistent procrastination, missing school or work, alienating friends and family, or performing badly in social or professional settings.

Other forms of fury include something known as "overwhelmed anger," which arises when a person feels like they are unable to deal with the pressures of everyday life.

ANGER THAT IS CAUSED BY THE INDIVIDUAL THEMSELVES, also known as "SELF-INFLICTED ANGER," may be a response to feelings of guilt and humiliation.

The emotion of JUDGMENTAL ANGER arises when we feel that we have been wronged or that someone else is lacking in some way.

Anger That Is Both Loud And Noisy

It is not always easy to convey our displeasure in the appropriate manner. We are permitted to display it assertively, either by letting other people know that we don't like the conduct or what they said, or by finding another safe outlet for our anger so that we don't stay irritated and angry all the time. In order to avoid suppressing it too much and giving it an overly bottled up appearance.

The difficulty is that the vast majority of us will choose the inappropriate means to vent our rage. Let's take a look at what happens when your anger is really loud and it begins to turn violent. In the following chapter, we will discuss what happens when you attempt to lessen violence and when you don't take care of it the way you should. For now, let's take a look at what happens when your anger is extremely loud and it starts to become violent.

Now, we have all been guilty of having these kind of outbursts on occasion. It's possible that we made an attempt to communicate our rage, or that we bottled it up for far too long and then made the rookie error of letting it all out. We can all admit it. Use it as a learning experience in proper anger management, and then put it behind you so you can go on with your life. It may not be the healthiest thing to do, but if you can only remember it occurring a few times in your whole life, it's probably not a big deal.

Explosions are often the only option for a person to let their rage out since they have no other outlet for it. They will reveal their passion whenever they get furious, which is most of the time. This will happen whenever they become angry. To convey their point of view, they are free to shout and scream, call others names, issue threats, beat and kick, and engage in a wide variety of other behaviors. This is often accompanied by some type of bullying, which, in the long run, will only serve to make the problem ten times more difficult to deal with.

This condition is often referred to as either an intermittent explosive disorder (IED) or an explosive anger disorder (EAD, respectively). These are the circumstances in which a person is more likely to have a potentially harmful outburst of rage, which is out of proportion to the stress that led to it being triggered in the first place. These outbursts will often not last for as long and will be accompanied by a variety of symptoms that we can see manifesting themselves in the body, such as profuse perspiration and spasms.

They are not doing themselves any favors by venting their rage in this manner; nonetheless, these individuals will discover that abusing others in this manner, regardless of the costs involved, will provide them with a feeling of comfort that their rage has been expelled. Additionally, they may experience pleasure on occasion as well.

This illness is become more common by the day, which is particularly concerning given the fact that many of the conventional strategies for dealing with stress and anger are now thought to be unhealthy. According to the findings of certain research, about 16 million people in the United States are affected by this ailment. However, we must keep in mind that there are a variety of methods to classify something, and that a standard has not yet been decided upon. It might be difficult to differentiate between those who are struggling with an angry outburst and those who would be diagnosed with emotional and behavioral disorders (EAD). In addition, in order to qualify as having this kind of disorder, explosive outbursts are required to take place in the absence of any other health conditions or psychological issues. This implies that if the individual is misusing chemicals and pharmaceuticals or is suffering with something like Alzheimer's, strictly speaking, they would not have EAD. [Citation needed]

Naturally, having this sort of impulsive outburst with your anger may make it tough to be social, which means that not as many people will want to be around you. This is because having these kinds of outbursts can make it difficult to be sociable. Additionally, there is a concern, shared by some individuals, about the potential for this conduct to become harmful and hazardous. Many people feel that EAD is the primary factor in incidents of traffic rage, large vandalism, domestic violence, and other types of violent altercations. People who are affected by this disease will have difficulty maintaining relationships and jobs, and they may be more likely to make snap judgments.

Think at it this way: Would you want to employ someone who has a lot of difficulties keeping their anger under control all the time? Would you prefer to have the constant worry that they could turn physically aggressive against you, other workers, or even customers, or that they might start ranting and raving at you?

Imagine how much more stressful it would be in a romantic relationship if this were a problem in the job. There would be a lot of talk about things that don't important, and you could be anxious about the other person's safety. You would never know what your position is with the other person. Therefore, the fact that many instances of domestic violence may be associated to someone with EAD demonstrates that being in a relationship is not safe for the person who is being abused by their spouse.

Why Is This Person So Angry?

There is a wide variety of possible triggers for EAD; however, the specific factors responsible are not yet completely known. There might be a few different reasons for this. People who are told that anger is bad or who are not taught how to appropriately control it may acquire this issue at some point in their life journey. There may be a connection between having a low serotonin turnover rate and this form of impulsive aggression, as shown by certain research; however, there may also be other factors at play.

The amounts of sugar in your blood have also been connected to EAD. It has been shown that individuals with EAD have increased insulin secretion, which would ultimately result in low blood sugar levels. On the other hand, if this were the only issue at play whenever anyone became angry, people would simply appease them by giving them a snack. There are situations in which individuals get irrationally furious when their blood sugar level is low, but in most cases, this behavior is related with other medical conditions. In most cases, the individual does not get the EAD designation while dealing with a situation of this kind.

Injuries to the prefrontal cortex are an additional issue that should be taken into consideration. The ability of people to prepare for the long term may be impacted as a result of this. since of this, they would have less capacity to foresee how their behavior would act, and since they are not thinking about some of the things that they are doing, this would result in outbursts that are impulsive and frequently harmful. This would indicate that they had less ability to control how their behavior would behave.

One good illustration of this would be the situation in which someone took too much. It will be tough for you to think clearly and make sound decisions if you drink alcohol because it will impair your judgment and make it harder for you to keep track of the many diverse behaviors you engage in on a daily basis. You do not want to associate EAD issues with alcohol usage, so if you have an anger problem that results in many violent outbursts, then it's time to seek some alcohol treatment if it's already a problem for you or to abstain from using it if it is not a problem for you. If you feel like you have an anger problem that results in many violent outbursts, then it's time to consider some alcohol treatment.

1. Choose a certain subject to discuss and a set time to do it.

Say what has to be spoken if there is a burdensome problem that needs to be handled with your spouse. Discuss the importance of setting aside some time to speak everything out. When discussing this matter, create an environment in which people are open and prepared to expose themselves to risk.

It is simple to adopt this position, but doing so will not advance the conversation, so make an effort to avoid becoming overbearing or opinionated. Keep in mind that the primary goal of this strategy is to put things out in the open in an uncomplicated manner. Be flexible when setting a date and time, and try to make everything as straightforward as possible. If you want to create a soothing environment while you figure out what's going on, try having your go-to beverage or cookie as you chat about it.

2. Keep on the subject at hand.

Having settled on a day and time for the meeting, continue with the business at hand. Although this may eventually lead to other topics, you should attempt to keep your attention on the one that is giving you the most trouble right now. Don't give in to the temptation of utilizing one issue as the ideal occasion to 'air your laundry' just so you may talk about anything else. I can tell you right now that this will only lead to pain and defensiveness, with no possible resolution in sight.

If the issue were to go off into a lengthy discussion about 'everything,' your conversation partner would feel as if they were fooled into accepting your offer to have a straightforward chat about 'one thing,' and they might become less receptive to your attempts to speak about anything in the future.

In the event that the situation begins to worsen, it is necessary to take a break for the time being. Explain that you are now experiencing a little of stress and that you think it would be best to continue this conversation at another time. Keep in mind that the purpose of this conversation is to address a problem, not to create new problems. It's okay, they are only some of the constraints that come with being human.

3. Get in the habit of practicing active listening

Conversation is enjoyable, but no one wants to sit through an extended monologue. Participate actively in the conversation that is going on. Participate in the discussion as well as nod your head, maintain eye contact, smile, and provide feedback. This feedback may be as easy as stating something along the lines of "I hear what you are saying, I understand, and I can see why this is upsetting."

On both ends, there must be communication, including verbal and nonverbal engagement with one another. Ask for some input every once in a while. Keep in mind that some individuals need to have their message coaxed out of silence before it can be heard by others. Be patient, and don't try to compel recognition; instead, just explain why it's necessary. You may try asking your spouse to rephrase what you are expressing in their own terms, according to how they understand it. It is important to remember not to take anything for granted. Everyone has their own unique point of view and perspective on a particular event or circumstance.

4. A middle ground

There is just no feasible way for all of our requirements to be fulfilled all of the time. This is how things really are. We are all aware of the situation...lol. It is a well-known truth that no two people are exactly alike; even identical twins exhibit some degree of individuality. When it comes to our romantic relationships, everyone of us is entitled to a certain amount of privacy. It is essential for partners in a relationship to be able to respect one another's personal space and to promote each other's ongoing emotional, mental, and physical development. We all deserve this in order to become better people as we go through the process of changing and progressing to higher levels in our lives. Keeping this in mind, you should expect reciprocity from your spouse as well.

Carry out some kind of self-evaluation, and be truthful with yourself about the results. Do you feel that it is important enough to actually put your foot down and refuse to make any concessions on the matter at hand? Check to see if there is a way for each of you to get your needs met on an individual basis, and if there is, choose to go down those paths rather than the ones that allow you to confidently get your own needs met as well. Think about the recurring themes of conflict that come up in your relationship, and take the time to investigate the origins of those conflicts to determine where the problem is stemming from. Disputes don't always revolve around the issues that "appear" to be at the heart of them. They often stem from far more fundamental requirements and yearnings, the nature of which may be unearthed and finally satiated by means of communication that is both loving and honest, as well as by planting the seeds of compromise.

There is a wide variety of possible triggers for EAD; however, the specific factors responsible are not yet completely known. There might be a few different reasons for this. People who are told that anger is bad or who are not taught how to appropriately control it may acquire this issue at some point in their life journey. There may be a connection between having a low serotonin turnover rate and this form of impulsive aggression, as shown by certain research; however, there may also be other factors at play.

The amounts of sugar in your blood have also been connected to EAD. It has been shown that individuals with EAD have increased insulin secretion, which would ultimately result in low blood sugar levels. On the other hand, if this were the only issue at play whenever anyone became angry, people would simply appease them by giving them a snack. There are situations in which individuals get irrationally furious when their blood sugar level is low, but in most cases, this behavior is related with other medical conditions. In most cases, the individual does not get the EAD designation while dealing with a situation of this kind.

Injuries to the prefrontal cortex are an additional issue that should be taken into consideration. The ability of people to prepare for the long term may be impacted as a result of this. since of this, they would have less capacity to foresee how their behavior would act, and since they are not thinking about some of the things that they are doing, this would result in outbursts that are impulsive and frequently harmful. This would indicate that they had less ability to control how their behavior would behave.

One good illustration of this would be the situation in which someone took too much. It will be tough for you to think clearly and make sound decisions if you drink alcohol because it will impair your judgment and make it harder for you to keep track of the many diverse behaviors you engage in on a daily basis. You do not want to associate EAD issues with alcohol usage, so if you have an anger problem that results in many violent outbursts, then it's time to seek some alcohol treatment if it's already a problem for you or to abstain from using it if it is not a problem for you. If you feel like you have an anger problem that results in many violent outbursts, then it's time to consider some alcohol treatment.

1. Choose a certain subject to discuss and a set time to do it.

Say what has to be spoken if there is a burdensome problem that needs to be handled with your spouse. Discuss the importance of setting aside some time to speak everything out. When discussing this matter, create an environment in which people are open and prepared to expose themselves to risk.

It is simple to adopt this position, but doing so will not advance the conversation, so make an effort to avoid becoming overbearing or opinionated. Keep in mind that the primary goal of this strategy is to put things out in the open in an uncomplicated manner. Be flexible when setting a date and time, and try to make everything as straightforward as possible. If you want to create a soothing environment while you figure out what's going on, try having your go-to beverage or cookie as you chat about it.

2. Keep on the subject at hand.

Having settled on a day and time for the meeting, continue with the business at hand. Although this may eventually lead to other topics, you should attempt to keep your attention on the one that is giving you the most trouble right now. Don't give in to the temptation of utilizing one issue as the ideal occasion to 'air your laundry' just so you may talk about anything else. I can tell you right now that this will only lead to pain and defensiveness, with no possible resolution in sight.

If the issue were to go off into a lengthy discussion about 'everything,' your conversation partner would feel as if they were fooled into accepting your offer to have a straightforward chat about 'one thing,' and they might become less receptive to your attempts to speak about anything in the future.

In the event that the situation begins to worsen, it is necessary to take a break for the time being. Explain that you are now experiencing a little of stress and that you think it would be best to continue this conversation at another time. Keep in mind that the purpose of this conversation is to address a problem, not to create new problems. It's okay, they are only some of the constraints that come with being human.

3. Get in the habit of practicing active listening

Conversation is enjoyable, but no one wants to sit through an extended monologue. Participate actively in the conversation that is going on. Participate in the discussion as well as nod your head, maintain eye contact, smile, and provide feedback. This feedback may be as easy as stating something along the lines of "I hear what you are saying, I understand, and I can see why this is upsetting."

On both ends, there must be communication, including verbal and nonverbal engagement with one another. Ask for some input every once in a while. Keep in mind that some individuals need to have their message coaxed out of silence before it can be heard by others. Be patient, and don't try to compel recognition; instead, just explain why it's necessary. You may try asking your spouse to rephrase what you are expressing in their own terms, according to how they understand it. It is important to remember not to take anything for granted. Everyone has their own unique point of view and perspective on a particular event or circumstance.

4. A middle ground

There is just no feasible way for all of our requirements to be fulfilled all of the time. This is how things really are. We are all aware of the situation...lol. It is a well-known truth that no two people are exactly alike; even identical twins exhibit some degree of individuality. When it comes to our romantic relationships, everyone of us is entitled to a certain amount of privacy. It is essential for partners in a relationship to be able to respect one another's personal space and to promote each other's ongoing emotional, mental, and physical development. We all deserve this in order to become better people as we go through the process of changing and progressing to higher levels in our lives. Keeping this in mind, you should expect reciprocity from your spouse as well.

Carry out some kind of self-evaluation, and be truthful with yourself about the results. Do you feel that it is important enough to actually put your foot down and refuse to make any concessions on the matter at hand? Check to see if there is a way for each of you to get your needs met on an individual basis, and if there is, choose to go down those paths rather than the ones that allow you to confidently get your own needs met as well. Think about the recurring themes of conflict that come up in your relationship, and take the time to investigate the origins of those conflicts to determine where the problem is stemming from. Disputes don't always revolve around the issues that "appear" to be at the heart of them. They often stem from far more fundamental requirements and yearnings, the nature of which may be unearthed and finally satiated by means of communication that is both loving and honest, as well as by planting the seeds of compromise.

MY CHILD REFUSES TO EVEN LISTEN!

The emphasis of this chapter will change from you, the parent, to your kid. Gaining an understanding of how to assist children with their difficult habits is a significant step in becoming a calm parent and bringing up a kid who is happy.

Now is the moment to educate yourself about your child's mental processes. Let's take a look at some instances of the many various sorts of actions that might damage a child's ability to control their rage. Which of these categories does your kid fit into?

THE CHILD WHO NEVER STOPS WAILING

When your child is inconsolable for extended periods of time, you could get the impression that you're going crazy. There are, however, a few different reasons why toddlers cry, which may help you comprehend the problem and find a way to deal with it.

The fact that toddlers are still learning how to articulate their requirements might be one of the reasons for all of the tantrums. They may not yet have the words to describe what they want or how they are feeling, so weeping may be the only way for them to communicate at this stage in their development.

Frustration is another typical factor that may lead to crying in toddlers. Toddlers are still developing their understanding of the world and their role in it; as a result, they are prone to experiencing frustration if their plans are thwarted. They could weep if they are unable to figure out how to perform something or if they are unable to express what it is that they desire.

In addition, toddlers are known to scream when they are in discomfort, exhausted, or hungry. All of these fundamental requirements have to be satisfied before a child may experience contentment and satisfaction in their environment.

In addition, some toddlers may just weep because they are unable to control the intensity of their feelings. They may be experiencing negative emotions such as sadness, fear, or anger but have no other means of expressing those sentiments.

You should bear in mind that a toddler sobbing is typically a natural aspect of growth, even if it may be unpleasant and tiring to cope with a child who is crying for no apparent reason.

Therefore, as a parent, should you try to prevent your child from crying?

No!

According to scientific research, some of the advantages include the following:

The release of stress hormones via crying is beneficial. On the other hand, holding back tears might raise levels of stress.

Both your blood pressure and your heart rate will decrease when you cry.

Crying helps remove certain toxins in your body that might build up due to emotional stress, such as having a hard day. These toxins could be eliminated from your body while you cry.

When exactly does an excessive amount of sobbing become unacceptable?

The fact that it is OK to weep means that it is okay for your kid to cry. On the other hand, it is not healthy for your youngster to have the misconception that rupturing a tear gland would automatically get them anything. To reiterate, if your kid constantly cries to attract your attention, you shouldn't always give in to their demands (provided that it is safe to do so). The word that's important here is "always." It is important that you pay attention to your kid the majority of the time. Nevertheless, they would learn an important lesson about life if they were not given this privilege every time, and that is that individuals do not always receive what they desire.

What should you do if your kid is weeping and you can't comfort them?

Check to see whether your kid is experiencing any kind of physical discomfort.

Make an effort to figure out why your kid is weeping. Is your kid hungry, irritable, lonely, or too tired? How about all four? Does your kid have HALT?

Keep your distance. You want your youngster to be aware that you are still there in the world. This may include giving your infant a comforting embrace, holding their palms, or keeping eye contact with them for a considerable amount of time.

You should make an effort to divert your toddler's attention with something else, such as a toy or staring out the window.

Get out of the atmosphere you're in right now and go for a stroll if you can.

Children are often receptive to having their minds changed by exposure to natural settings.

4. Having an understanding of the ways in which anger is expressed

The emotion of anger doesn't necessarily have a negative connotation. Many experts in the field who research anger are of the opinion that the emotion may be useful and even contribute to good results in the workplace provided it is controlled and communicated in an appropriate manner. Enhancements to interpersonal connections and lines of communication, as well as advancements in operational procedures and other beneficial shifts at work, might be among the positive results.

Mark Gorkin, a certified clinical social worker, is an anger expert who holds the belief that there are beneficial and useful uses for rage. A model that Gorkin has developed to assist investigate and explain how anger is conveyed has been created by Gorkin. In the first part of his discussion, he draws a distinction between the value of expressing anger and the motive behind doing so.

The display of rage may have either a productive or harmful purpose, depending on how it is used. Furthermore, the manifestation of rage may be either planned or spontaneous, depending on the speaker's state of mind.

You may find out more about what each expression linked with usefulness and intention implies for the display of rage by selecting each one individually.

Effortless to put together

Constructive anger expression occurs when the speaker maintains their own integrity and ideals while still showing respect for others around them. This is mostly an objective and logical reaction to the rage that was experienced by the individual.

A destructive force

When anger is expressed in a manner that is damaging, it has a tendency to become more personal and amplified. It is impacted by a person's frailties and shows a lack of regard for the people around them.

To the point

An deliberate manifestation of one's anger is a purposeful reaction to that anger. Both the manner in which one's anger will be conveyed and the result that is sought need some level of consideration. This requires a great deal of restraint on your part.

Unplanned or unexpected.

Anger that is expressed on the spur of the moment is a knee-jerk reaction that leaves little room for either planning or reflecting on possible subsequent actions. Self-control is not present to the same extent as it is with deliberate expression.

Think on it.

Is the rage that you express productive or destructive when it comes to its potential effects? Is it more common for you to vent your anger in a spontaneous manner or on purpose?

Consider the ways in which you vent your rage, and then write down your thoughts in the area given. When you are done, use the box labeled Next Page to continue learning about the ways in which people show their anger.

Your answer may either be written down or entered into a text file in the program you use for your word processor (or in a text editor such as Notepad), and then the file can be saved to your hard disk for later reading.

It's possible that you'll show anger in various ways depending on the circumstances: sometimes in a productive and intentional manner, and other times possibly more destructively and on the spur of the moment. Going back to Gorkin's model for a moment, when you combine the factors of usefulness and intention, you get a wide variety of results, some of which are more favorable than others. Purposeful and constructive, purposeful and destructive, spontaneous and constructive, and spontaneous and destructive are the four possible combinations.

After doing so, Gorkin chooses a single phrase to characterize the manifestation of rage that emerges as a consequence of integrating each of the separate ways of expressing fury. When rage is combined with utterances that have a goal and are constructive, Gorkin uses the term assertion to characterize the resulting emotion.

The act of expressing one's anger while keeping in mind the need of finding a solution that is beneficial is referred to as assertion. Self-control enables a person to maintain composure and reason while asserting themselves, providing an explanation for why they are furious and what steps need to be taken to calm them down. During this time, there is an emphasis placed on respecting the beliefs and viewpoints held by others, which enhances the probability of a positive settlement being reached. When you are trying to let your anger out at work, you should always make it a point to be as aggressive as possible.

Anger that is directed against others and has a harmful intent is often the result of a person's weaknesses. According to Gorkin, the best term to characterize the interaction between these two is "hostility." When someone is hostile, they are often defending themselves, and their aim, whether conscious or not, is to attack or seek revenge. This approach is not a very helpful method of addressing the issue that initially caused the anger to arise in the first place.

Expressions of hostile rage are frequently accompanied by the use of blame, judgment, or accusations that are intended to induce feelings of guilt in the target. This kind of rage often finds expression in conduct that might be described as passive-aggressive. At the very least, you should refrain from showing your aggressive rage at the workplace.

What Is It?

Try to match the many ways of expressing anger with the attributes linked with them. There is a possibility that more than one characteristic will be matched to each expression type.

Alternate Meanings:

A. Directed toward achieving goals and productive B. On purpose and with a harmful intent

To accomplish:

1. Requires the use of assertions 2. Is devoid of respect 3. Has a propensity to be too personal and dramatic 1. 4. Attempt to find a solution

A response

The state of having asserted oneself is one in which one's anger has been expressed in a way that is both deliberate and helpful in response.

Regrettably, disrespectful reactions to rage include those that are purposefully damaging. The hatred that is generated might make it difficult to find a solution to the rage and achieve any kind of positive result.

Anger often manifests itself in very individualized and exaggerated ways that are intended to cause harm to others. Because of this, attaining beneficial consequences after feelings of wrath is difficult, if not impossible.

The goal is to find a solution while maintaining a courteous and thoughtful attitude. The combination of these two expressions, "purposeful and constructive," is likely to result in consequences that are both positive and productive.

Anger That Is Channeled In A Positive Way

There are numerous subtleties to inappropriate manifestations of anger, and the majority of them sit within the three regions that we have described. However, there are many additional alternatives that fall somewhere in between these three categories. There are, however, only two healthy methods to express anger in a constructive way: being aggressive and being prepared to let go if being assertive does not work.

Unwavering confidence: Start with this when you are feeling furious. While we are going to delve into how to handle particular circumstances, here is where you should begin being angry, and this is where you should finish becoming hopeful. A healthy instinct to protect our needs, self-worth, values, and convictions is at the root of anger, and expressing your anger helps you keep these things intact while also respecting and taking into consideration the needs, self-worth, values, and convictions of the person who disturbed your constitution and caused you to become angry.

Relationships flourish, maturity advances, and peace of mind prevails when one deals with anger in a manner that is authoritative but polite, all while maintaining a tone of good humour. Being obstinate, dominant, rude, and unpleasant are not characteristics of assertiveness; rather, they are indicators of an aggressive demeanor that is visible to others. They are not gestures of love in the family, they do not contribute to a great energy environment at work, and they will only do damage.

The following are some examples of ways that you might express your anger:

If you feel like you have too much on your plate, you might ask for assistance or ask to have some responsibilities taken off your plate. In addition, if you already have more work than you are able to do, you may respectfully decline any more work that is offered to you.

When you are feeling overwhelmed or fatigued, you always have the option to courteously request a break to relax or meditate. This is true regardless of the circumstances.

If you are going to be spending an excessive amount of time with extended relatives or a social scene of friends, you have the right to gently seek some space and solitude from time to time.

You can have a civil conversation with your significant other about the divergent paths your lives may take, or you can have a conversation with your coworkers about the divergent approaches they take to their jobs, without having to compromise your principles or try to coerce someone into altering their point of view.

The slate stays clean and there are no grudges to bear when there is consistent assertiveness and team play. However, you should constantly keep in mind the importance of being selective with your assertiveness; otherwise, it will lose its power.

Getting Over Your Angry Feelings: The idea of "letting go" may seem to be extremely easy and practical, but in practice, it is far more challenging than being aggressive. This is particularly true in a world where society frowns upon signs of weakness and celebrates displays of strength. Everyone has the same goal: to win! Our culture mocks those who just up and leave! What does this imply about the fury that engulfs our society? If being politely aggressive does not change the course of events, then the best course of action is to "let the anger go." Believe it or not, this is the better alternative, and it is rich with STRENGTH, when a strong and polite approach does not work, and it is ready to go.

When you let go of your anger, you are acknowledging that you are unable to exert total control over every circumstance and that you are aware of the limitations of what you can do to alter the consequences. It also implies that the joy and contentment you experience in your own life have nothing to do with the decisions made by another individual. It is by no means a failure on any level. You come out ahead as a result.

Lastly, letting go and moving on to the next stage of forgiving someone is not the same thing as suppressing anger. It's a good way to let out some of that fury. It has to be genuine, and it can't have any ill will against anybody.

You Can Help Your Children Better Manage Their Anger By Teaching Them Self-Control.

Self-control is the capacity to keep one's cool in the face of adversity and the skill of pausing to consider one's options before taking action. It is being conscious of both your internal and external experiences. This is an idea that has to be conveyed to students and put into practice. In the following, we will discuss some of the measures you can take to help your kid learn healthy ways to deal with anger:

You should try to get your children to speak about their experiences with things that make them angry.

Children have a limited capacity to comprehend their own feelings; nevertheless, when they communicate those feelings to an adult, they may have a deeper understanding of those feelings. Encourage your kid to discuss everything that's going on, and listen to what they have to say without passing judgment.

Wait to pass judgment and make evaluations until they have completed, and then gently guide them to identify the particular feeling. Talk to the kid about how they handled the situation, and together think of some other, more positive ways that they may have responded to the situation. Instead of giving her orders to change her behavior, try reaching a compromise with her.

Recognize and get a handle on your emotions.

When children are unable to comprehend the emotions that they are experiencing, it may be challenging for them to articulate the experiences that provoke anger in them. As a result, it is our responsibility to steer our children safely through this. When we guide children through the process of recognizing these sensations via practice, it will be much simpler for them to know what to do when they experience these particular feelings.

Reading children's books may be a helpful approach to get a knowledge of and articulate a variety of emotions. It's possible that varied facial expressions correspond to distinct emotions on their faces. You as a parent or guardian may concentrate on each and ask your kid what sensation each one is, as well as ask your child to show you the expression on his or her face when they are experiencing that emotion.

Ask the kid to give you examples of times when he felt that way and what led up to him or her feeling that way in the first place. Also, ask the youngster what led up to him or her feeling that way. You may next describe a successful method to respond to a circumstance that is either identical to the one you just experienced or one that is quite close to it.

Show some empathy.

While you are working to educate your kid to constructively express their anger, you should strive to understand what it is like for them by putting yourself in their position. It should be your goal to raise children that respect and learn from you rather than despise you. Someone speaking to you in the same manner that you talk to your children should not make you uncomfortable since doing so will be done out of respect for your children as well.

Take some time off.

It is essential that we teach our children the importance of taking a break from activities or situations that cause them stress. Instruct them on how to achieve the status of S.T.A.R. This means to either smile or stop for a moment; then take a big breath and unwind.

When someone is nervous, terrified, or furious, their breathing becomes extremely shallow, and their heartbeat increases in rate. For this reason, it is recommended to take slow, deep breaths, since this increases the amount of oxygen that is supplied to the brain.

You may also assist your kid find a secure location where they can go to get away from an irritating atmosphere or circumstance by using your resources. When you are both in a secure location, you should make an effort to communicate your requirements to the other person in as clear and concise a manner as possible.

An illustration of this would be to tell him that his face is creased and unpleasant, then show him how it appears, and then tell him that you will be ready to travel with him as soon as his face has relaxed more.

Give your kid a say in the matters that concern them.

Make it feasible for your youngster to have a say in the decisions that are being made or the sequence of the events that are taking place. If your kid is hesitant to always clean his teeth before going to bed, one helpful example would be to inform him that it is his bedtime when he expresses this reluctance.

However, you should inquire as to whether or not he would like to put on his pajamas or clean his teeth first. This is a great way of conveying that both activities are necessary, but it has a brilliant twist in which your kid has been empowered to chose which activity he wants to undertake first. This is a clever way of communicating that both activities are mandatory, but it has a lovely twist.

It is essential that you do not give in to all of the outbursts and tantrums that are being thrown. No matter how humiliating the circumstance may be, you must remember to keep your cool as a parent. You are not have to give in to your child's demands and purchase him sweets if, for instance, they start weeping in a shop because they want candy and you are in that store.

You are nonetheless able to provide the youngster with another option. You may show compassion for him or her by acknowledging that you are aware of their tears and letting them know that you understand why it is that you were unable to buy her chocolates. After you have finished explaining why you did not buy her the candy, offer her another choice, such as apples or bananas, to choose from after you have finished your explanation.

Instill in your youngster the understanding that every action has both a reward and a consequence.

Clearly describe the repercussions that will follow any improper conduct. If your kid does anything that you consider to be inappropriate, you should correct them and explain to them why their behavior is inappropriate. You should also use this opportunity to convey to him the consequences of making the same mistake again.

One illustration of this would be the scenario in which your youngster slaps his brother because of a toy. Explain to him that it is unacceptable to beat his brother in order to get access to a toy for himself. Then you should tell him that he will not be allowed to use the toy again if he continues to strike the other person.

Ask him whether he understood what you were saying, and then wait for a response to see whether or not he agrees with what you have to say. If he continues to strike his brother, you should prevent him from using the item until he apologizes.

Awards That Are Appropriate

In the same way that you should make sure to deliver penalties, you should also give positive reinforcement. Your goal should be to encourage your kid to continue displaying positive behaviors by rewarding him for each one he does. You may improve the probability that a particular good behavior will be repeated by a youngster by providing praise and attention to it after it has occurred.

Set an example for the proper conduct.

Always keep in mind what we covered before, which is that your actions are the finest example you can provide to your kid. Educate yourself about appropriate conduct, particularly with regard to how you should respond when placed in difficult circumstances and how you should behave while furious. It is simple for a youngster to pick up on the appropriate conduct by seeing their parents. Having the ability to educate students how to keep their cool in trying circumstances is a valuable teaching skill.

If you have misplaced your vehicle keys, for instance, you should first collect yourself and then enlist the assistance of your children in looking for the keys. If, despite all of your frantic attempts, you are unable to locate the keys, you should let your children know that you are going to take a few deep breaths and play back the events of the last few minutes in an effort to find out where you put the keys.

This should be done before you continue the search. The children may learn from this experience that the best way to deal with frustrating circumstances is to remain level-headed and composed.

Advancing One Step Further: The Effects And Cautionary Notes

It doesn't matter whether you're fuming because your colleagues don't know how to perform their jobs properly, because your relationships are always falling apart, or because you're just sticking up for yourself when you believe you've been treated unfairly; the fact remains that your life is being negatively affected by your tendency to feel and express excessive anger. It is necessary to exercise some kind of command over it before it gets out of hand. Keep in mind that the fact that you need to exercise self-control over your anger does not imply that you are in the wrong; it is possible that your emotions are warranted. It only indicates that you have discovered a more effective approach to deal with the circumstances and that you are not allowing wrath to take control of your life.

Why bother looking for an alternative when your anger serves its purpose of getting things done and keeping others in check just fine? The answer to this question is the significant amount of harm that it is causing to your life in a variety of various areas and contexts.

The Effects of Having an Angry Attitude Emotional – There is no denying the influence that rage has on one's mental state. You have just yelled at someone over a little error that they committed while carrying out a job that you assigned to them. Because of your yelling, they were able to find a solution to the situation, and the work went off without a hitch. Having said that, you could be concentrating on the incorrect issue at this juncture. Right now is the time for you to take a moment to reflect and ask yourself, "How do you feel?" Do you have a sense of inner calm, or do you often experience feelings of restlessness and agitation? Even though they seem to be fleeting at the present time, the negative impacts on your mental state that are left behind by rage might prove to be rather detrimental in the long term.

You may not be able to control yourself, you may not feel mentally stable, and you may feel emotionally tired all the time. These are just a few of the indicators that the toll your wrath is having on your life is becoming apparent. Can you remember of a moment when you had a disagreement with someone, and it wrecked not just your mood but also the rest of your day? You were short-tempered with everyone and were unable to concentrate on other activities without being quickly upset. Get rid of this emotional reaction that wrath instills in you so that it doesn't become chronic and make irritation a part of who you are before it becomes.

Physical - Perhaps you believe that the emotional repercussions of anger are normal and that you do not need to let go of it because you are good at managing your emotions. You may also believe that you do not need to let go of it because you are physically capable of doing so. However, this complicated sensation will not cease to have an effect on your life at this point. Due to their inability to manage their emotions, those who have issues with aggressiveness have a greater chance of developing cardiovascular disease as well as having an increased likelihood of experiencing a heart attack or stroke. Anger is associated with an increase in stress, which in turn may lead to headaches, high blood pressure, chronic tiredness, and a number of other physical diseases that can significantly disturb your day-to-day life.

If you have ever been on the receiving end of someone else's extreme fury, you are well aware of the toll it takes on the quality of your connection with those you care about. Anger issues in a marriage often result in a frustrating cycle that begins with a trigger, moves on to an angry outburst, is followed by remorse, frustration, and then begins again with the trigger. No matter how terrible you feel after an angry outburst, it may be almost hard for you to express this to the person you have a crucial relationship with. Other social interactions, such as those at your place of employment, will also suffer if your professional and formal relationships are handled badly and are exclusively based on fear or authority.

It is important that you be aware that anger, even if it is not aimed at the children that you are raising or want to raise, may have a direct impact on their upbringing. This is true even if the anger is not directed at the children. Children who have been raised in a hostile environment have a greater propensity to demonstrate the same behavior as adults, to acquire psychotic tendencies, and to participate in illegal activities.

Because neither response is proper or healthy, it is essential to have the ability to manage your emotions to the extent that you can choose a different response to a given situation. You will never need to worry about the destruction that rage can wreak on your life again if you are able to understand what causes you to get angry and put a stop to the anger as soon as it starts to build up inside of you.

In tense situations, stepping away from the conflict is often the best and healthiest response one can have. Spend a few minutes trying to gather your thoughts, calming down, and figuring out where your feelings are coming from. Meditation and other mindfulness practices often work well at this time of day.

If you are seeking a solution to outbursts that will last for a longer period of time, you should try to find healthy methods to frequently express the anger that you may feel via physical exercise. Participate in organized sports or boxing classes at a local gym, for example.

It is essential that you make daily efforts to cultivate mindfulness practices.

Maintain a journal in which you record how you are feeling at certain times and why. Try your hand at meditation, or sign up for some yoga sessions. Perform frequent physical activity. Make sure that you give yourself plenty of time to engage in "self-care," even if "self-care" consists of nothing more than taking a relaxing bath and reading a book. Find a local counselor or psychologist to consult with if you feel that these simple ways of practicing mindfulness are not adequate. They may be able to offer you with further assistance to manage your emotions and stress, or they may supply you with medicine that might help you. Both of these options may be available to you.

The most essential thing for you to keep in mind, though, is that anger is exacerbated by stress. Because your stress levels are already high and your body is already full of those dreadful stress chemicals, whether you are upset about anything that is going on at work or at home, you are much more likely to feel rage. This is because your stress levels are already high.

7. Get some exercise.

It is time to make some adjustments to your lifestyle if you are someone who struggles with anger on a constant basis and who seems to be nearing the boiling point very often. These changes will help you achieve greater outcomes and will help you feel better overall. And beginning an exercise routine is one of the finest things that you can do to assist yourself in this situation.

Endorphins are chemicals that are produced in the body when someone begins an exercise regimen on a regular basis. These endorphins are wonderful since they will assist the body in becoming less anxious as a result of their presence. Because of this, it is reasonable to assert that engaging in regular physical activity is one of the best ways to keep fury and other negative emotions under control.

There is a wide variety of physical activity that you may include into your daily routine in order to acquire the recommended amount of physical activity and to stimulate the production of endorphins. The following are examples of some of these activities:

Jogging and Boxing Exercises

In the water

The practice of martial arts

Hoops and baskets

Cycling while doing yoga

Working out with weights and running

It is recommended that you make an effort to obtain some kind of physical activity at least a couple times each week. Working exercise three to four times a week, or even more, for approximately thirty minutes at a time will provide you with a lot of great health benefits and will really assist you in gaining better control of your anger.

www.ingramcontent.com/pod-product-compliance
Lightning Source LLC
Chambersburg PA
CBHW050414120526
44590CB00015B/1966